# INTERNAL

# INTERNAL

**Corporal Christian Vanderbush** served in the United States Marine Corps Reserve from 2013 to 2019. Christian served as an Infantry Marine and deployed to Afghanistan in support of Operation Freedom's Sentinel in 2017 through 2018.

He maintained a love of writing from a young age that developed into a cathartic method of expressing feeling through verse. This method began to take form in earnest while he perused a bookstore nestled in the corner of Ireland's Shannon Airport, the last stop for many American service members headed for destinations in the Middle East and Southeast Asia. He was experiencing the excitement, anticipation, and expected nerves of his first deployment when he discovered a collection of poetry by famed Irish poet W.B. Yeats. After several hours tearing through the pages, he took out a notebook and wrote the first of many poems that would be a welcome reprieve from the rigors of deployment.

Internal is a collection of some of those poems written while deployed and during his first year home. This collection is a deeply personal dive into dark places Veterans like Corporal Vanderbush often feel the need to hide. He hopes this collection spreads his all-important message: its ok to have these feelings and you are not alone.

# INTERNAL

Christian
Vanderbush

**BOST**
**BOOKS**
Sт. Johns, MI

INTERNAL
Copyright © 2020 by Christian Vanderbush

Cover photo by Christian Vanderbush
Author photo by USMC Corporal Nick Durst

First Bost Books edition - November 2020

ISBN: 978-0-578-79446-4

dedication

# For Bangarang.

# AFGHANISTAN 17-18

## Poems on Post

## Musings

# FIRST YEAR HOME

## Relearning

# AFGHANISTAN 17-18

# Poems
# on Post

# GRIN

---

Ain't shit we can do but grin and bear it.

Wear the bullshit like a crown,

Pass it around and choke it down.

Fake a laugh and beg time pass,
Ignore the slow toil of the hourglass.

Drown the ticking of the clock.

Ain't shit we can do but hide the pain Until we board
that fucking plane.

# A HAIKU

---

It's one thirty here

It is four o'clock back home

Still nine hours ahead

# CULTURE SHOCK

How can a place so beautiful be so troubled? How can a culture so rich find so much to fight over?

Is it them?

Or is it us?

# THE FARMER

The Farmer wakes and sets to his task

To toil and sow, to plow and grow

Food for his family, feed for his goats

Pulling a living from the ground

Row after Row after Row

The Sun sets and the Sun rises, and the Farmer still
tends to his task

The Farmer doesn't have time to care about Jihadists or
the Governments they try to overthrow

# ALL IS WELL

All is well, All is well

Standing in the dark, surrounded by light

No one hears the falling tree, cracking branches exploding bark

All is well, All is well

Walking in the bitter lonely cold, chased by crowded heat

A race to cross the finish line, to reach the end and never grow old

All is well, All is well

High on a balcony far above the world, I've never felt closer to the ground

Looking out over my gnarled garden that begs for the shelter of a cloud

All is well, All is well

# VIGILANCE

Heavy eyes tell the littlest lies

But make no mistake:

Fail to listen and everyone dies

Movement in the darkness, a rustle of leaves

If you don't take them seriously

A family back home grieves

Watch for the enemy from dusk until dawn

Wait for the attack until you pick up and move on

I wonder how we'll ever stop

# FOR ME

---

I write poetry that rarely rhymes for people who couldn't care less.

I write with senseless rhythm because my crowd doesn't think it really matters.

When my work is recited aloud the audience is apathetic to my voice, its tone, and all its inflections.

On the stage that resides in the hollows of my soul I am the producer, lead act, biggest fan, and harshest critic.

Even though I collect each one of my words like an abstract obsession, I am aware I write for an uncaring, disinterested audience of one.

An audience of me.

# PUBLIC RELATIONS

Woo-da-ray-ga Na-day-wilam*

The magic words

Permission to kill him

Stop and Comply or you'll have to die

Blood in the sand and a hole for an eye

Even if he understood, do you think he knew why?

---

*     "wadarega yaa dee wulim" is a Pashto phrase loosely translating
to "Stop, Or I will Shoot."

# THE BEST

---

Trained to kill

Groomed to fight

Put on the wall to hold back the night

Try to remember the enemy is

The enemy

Not the idiots

In charge of me

Knowing if I die it's because

They can't get it right

Sheer incompetence

Will be the death of me

# 9,000 MILES

From 9,000 miles away

    I see your frustration

    I feel your pain

From 9,000 miles away

    I giftwrap my love and send it your way

    I know the words on screen aren't the same

From 9,000 miles away

    We fight together through the worst life offers

    We push forward with all we have to see the day

    that I am no longer 9,000 miles away

# AGAIN

Silence on post offers time for reflection. Time and solitude to contemplate life's direction. Are you the hero or are you the villain? Life, the grand competition. Ask yourself: you got what it takes to win?

Do you want to win? Repeat the question.

Again, again, again.

Saints and sinners, losers and winners. Run through life, stand post in a trance. Envy new lovers dancing their dance for beginners. Have you earned the right to be among them?

Do you want to be? Repeat the question.

Again, again, again.

How much have you loved? How much have you hated? When you meet St. Peter will he let you in? Remember the community he stands outside of is gated.

Do you want in? Repeat the question.

Again, again, again.

# MY HEROES

I admire these men only a few years older than I.
My senior year, I chased tail; these men were already
here, fighting this war and doing their best to make a
difference. Now they're back again, those who could
stomach a return. There are no better souls than these
for which I'd lay down my life,

the older brothers I never had, the older souls I was
blessed to follow into this war-torn land. They are the
finest of men though they'd never claim it.

If together, we all descend into Hell, there would be no
better company

though none of them deserve to ever make that
descent.

# RIDER

When the Bird comes crashing in,

Bringing with it chaos on the wind,

Watch for the calm man when it all begins.

He'll stand ready with a rifle in hand,

He'll stand silent with no delusions of the grand.

He'll greet the pale horse and call its' rider Friend.

With a wink and a marrow grin, they'll set out riding
side by side

And to only Death will he confide.

When the Reaper comes calling, the righteous
need not worry.

The wicked will flee from the reaper's companion,
a rider named Fury.

When chaos stirs and darkness looms,

The pale horse and its rider will call on their Friend.

Death brings with it the stoic man who
carries Hell within.

# MORE

We are so much more than Black and White

So much more than the things clouding our sight

One day our hearts will clear, and we'll make it through with time

Until then we will fight and fight and fight

To survive this treacherous night.

# NO ILLUSIONS

---

I hear what you are saying

I nod because I understand

I don't reply because I see

The things you say

The things you do

I don't reply because I see

The real you

# THE POET

Fear the Poet and the weapons he carries. Violence
of action alone can't kill him. All the bullets, bombs,
and sabers rattling in the world can't bring him down
and they know it. Ideas can't be killed, only ignored.
Try to shout them down and drown them out with
explosions; as the smoke clears, a whisper on the wind
will scream, "I'm still here."

I'm still here.

Year after year, I crawl out the crater. I know people
still hear. The Poet's ideas, the Poet's dreams. Commit
to verse the fire from the tongue, imbed it in the mind.
The idea, the dream, more permanent than death of
any kind. Peace, I cry; peace, I plead. Fight the good
fight, wage the good war, attempt to keep score when
peace is what we really need. Thump the holy book,
claim the holy land. Pull the trigger, drop the bomb,
claim to know the divine plan. Scream and scream
again. Tell us victory is one more puddle of blood in
the sand. Fear the Poet and the weapons he carries.
Fear his words travelling through eternity. Fear the
peace he screams:

I'M STILL HERE.

# THREE MORE MONTHS

Nine thousand miles
and three more months away

I can already feel your touch

I can already smell your hair

If I listen hard enough,
I can already hear you say,

"Welcome home, Marine, it's safe,
you're here to stay."

# SITREP, OVER.

We all joined to serve our country, a country that doesn't know or doesn't care we're here.

But other than that…

Everything is fine, Sir.

You asked us to prove ourselves to the Corps, but when we try, you send in the Army. We're not actually meant to do anything here, are we?

But other than that…

Everything is fine, Sir.

You sent in the Reserves because of our wide range of no particular skill set, yet I think you forgot to issue a crucial piece of gear. I think it's called Respect.

But other than that…

Everything is fine, Sir.

You're asking us to keep everyone safe with one arm behind our back and zero initiative to prevent an attack.

But other than that…

Everything is fine, Sir.

The Taliban knows our plans and that's just our luck because we've got advisors that just don't give a fuck.

But other than that…

Everything is fine, Sir.

The Marines got bored when they learned they wouldn't be fighting off a Jihadi hoard.

But other than that…

Everything is fine, Sir.

We just want to do our job, Sir.

But instead we're stuck on a FOB, Sir.

Other than that…

Everything is fine, Sir.

# NEWS

---

We're a forty-five second segment
on the midnight news

A page-6 Op-ed tucked away
next to last night's numbers

A meme that can't quite make enough people
feel guilty

Not forgotten, certainly good enough
for a slow news day

# thank you for your service

Standing watch but I see nothing

Listen till I can hear the nothing

Stand and watch, feel nothing but the brain rot

Withering away, withering away, withered away

Find solace in watching night fade to day

Then find sleep and sleep it all away

Gratitude, have to earn it.

Gratitude, do I deserve it?

Does gratitude make it all worth it?

Drop bombs for gratitude,

Stand post for peace

Am I making a difference?

Should we still be in the Middle East?

I don't fucking know

But I'll sip the Kool-Aid for ABC.

# AFGHANISTAN 17-18

# Musings

It makes sense if you don't
think about it.

# FROM A TREE

Never waste paper.

A tree ceased to grow

Because you had a message

You wanted the whole world to know

Honor a tree.

Be heard

Be heard

# DRUGS

I wonder if there's a word for the urge to walk
into the woods and never return

To clean your slate and fade away cloaked in
green and freed of grey

I wonder if there's peace deep in the trees
welcomed by the weeds, the leaves, the bees

What cure exists that heals the mind and helps
the soul stir,

If not for the soil that blankets the earth

Cleanse who you were and learn who you are
by bottling the wind and inhaling the stars

Whisper to the pines your human affair, the drug
of release that is fresh air

# HOME

I crave a home with a forest within its walls.

With beds of pine needles and willow switch halls.

I dream of cedar shake shingles, wildflower windows,
and blooms year-round hidden from snow.

Beneath a canopy of glass, a creek runs through,
carrying life to everything that grows.

I'll sleep in the ferns and eat with the trees
and pull from the soil all I can learn.

I wish to escape this drywall hell, this off-white
prison cell.

But something keeps me here, too unpleasant
to be 'kin to a weed.

That fabric blossom seeded in greed keeps me bolted
to incandescent iron bars.

I hate it here.

# CASTLE

It's a part of my whole; it's who I am, this
gaping hole in me.

But that's not the whole story, this empty space
in the middle.

There are frayed edges and cracked
foundations still holding my soul erect.

There are burning passions that arch to the sky,
holding remnants of stained windows with history
emblazoned on their lips.

Moss and ferns, soil and roots overgrew the floorboards
where visitors thudded and
tramped and scraped their way in and out of me.

Tapestries that whispered ill-kept secrets are
tucked in my corners, next to portraits of
sweet-tasting memories.

The roof may leak, and the hearth lays cold,
but my rubble and my ruins still have more
stories to be told.

# FREEDOM

---

I sometimes reflect on how much I've changed and realize how little changing I've actually done. I've experienced luxuries and horrors and often forget which is which, but at the end of the day, I'm still me. People say I'm a different person but it's always different people that never stay. How much can their opinion really mean anyway? Especially because the only constant is the same me, in different scenes, in different places, doing different things. Maybe I have changed. But what's that mean when nothing stays the same?

It means no one knows and no one really cares so fuck it, imma keep doing me:

It's my Independence Day.

# CIRCLES

Lost in a thirst trap because there's no roadmap
to escape loneliness in crowded rooms and the dread
that they might empty too soon.

Too soon to say hello and not enough time before
goodbye. So, I lie and I lie and I lie, seeking someone
who isn't hiding yet doesn't want to be found. I run
around and around and around till I've worn a path in
the ground.

Look at me but not too close. You might not
like what's around my corners and in my closets and
on my mind

It might look like a mirror and it's too hard to explain.
So, I deflect and evade and run away
and leave the truth in my wake.

A sinner and an angel make love and the world begins
to quake. I beg the aftershock never stop
so I can hide in its chaos, never witnessing foundations
settled in broken heaps.

But let's be honest: this is all a bad dream till I wake
and it repeats.

# SOCIAL

Sit pretty for the photo op

Wait for the flash

And don't forget your lines


Fight the war with a keyboard and a phone

Fire cyclic rate into cyberspace

Our social battle ground, the war of our times

# GOONS

Wolves sing to the moon and coyotes laugh in its light. But the monsters within worship the White Queen of the night.

Beasts of darkness cower in fear when they hear the black harpy circling near. But the devils and goons silently cheer and show their delight with their green-eyed sneer. They come and they go on their reaper's chore. Ice in their veins and fire in their core. Dancing in the moonlight to their bitter steel snicker, quenching their lust in pools of sweet ichor. The White Queen adores her flock of frenzied ghouls, her children of angels who refused to be ruled.

# ORIGIN STORY

Pity, she said, when she came to call. I look forward to none, but you least of all. How far you've fallen, weak, bloodied, and raw. But even the best can't avoid when I call. Lay still and breathe easy, let go of your fear. I've come now to take you; your time is near.

But he snarled and spat and fought to his feet. He screamed through his pain: I will not retreat. Take no offence, sweet matron of death; I beg you, please, leave me one last breath. While my brothers fight, my brothers live and if my brothers fight, I have more to give.

She pondered a moment, among death's rot. Give you shall, but live, you will not. She lifted him up and draped him in black and little by little, his skin began to crack. Leave your body behind, let your flesh fall away. Abandon who you were, this is where you stay. Death until death, pain until pain. You will be by my side when they call you brother again. You will be by my side when they call out your name. You will be my reaper, Protector of the Slain.

# TO QUARTERS

A checkered hull, a checkered hull

Here's to Lord Admiral Nelson,

Here's to the Old Bastard's fall

Fair Wind and Following Sheets

To Quarters! To Quarters!

The drummer boy beats

A cannon's roar and flight of Devils' ball

Here's to Lord Admiral Nelson,

Here's to the Old Bastard's fall

Onward! Straight at them!

Pray the Devil eat their wind

Don't dance and don't dawdle

Let the Lord find Victor in the Din

A checkered Hull, a checkered Hull!

Here's to Lord Admiral Nelson

Here's to the Old Bastard's Fall!

# FUCK

Ginsberg the quack

And looney bird Kerouac

Oh, what'd you do, oh, what'd you do

When you made the whole world listen to you?

You stirred the meek and gathered the wild.

What could anyone do

When the world embraced its new problem child?

The church cried out, the courts put you on trial.

Vulgar and lewd. Offensive and crude.

You did the world a favor when you called it a prude.

Free the body and unleash the mind,

Live truly free and the world will follow in kind.

Generations have passed with new writers to the task.

But alas, tragedy struck when the old writers passed the buck.

They forgot to teach that freedom meant more than the word "Fuck!"

---

Clinging to shackles and embracing tyrants,

Forgetting bondage was more than tight leather surprises.

Of course, it gets you erect; you live with a ball gag called politically correct.

Freedom's discomfort, but a dose of corruption made it less surreal.

Ended up addicted and corporate, finding home back on the hamster wheel.

It will only be us at fault

When we forget why we commit words to paper, press rubber to asphalt.

# WHY

Raindrops on my window

Wind whispering by

Thank you for waking me

Thank you for a grey sky

I am grateful you are gentle

I am grateful you are mine

I am grateful for today

This moment trapped in time

Raindrops on my window

Wind whispering by

Thank you for reminding me

Of why.

# SUNLIGHT

We often overlook the power of sunlight

In our search for remedies
And solutions, caught in the sweet honey

Of our beds, trapped in the soft embrace of sleep

We chase happiness in one more hour of rest

Forgetting day after day the remedy

Rises and falls whether we want it to or not

Only to remember its power when we see its light and feel its warmth on our chest.

# FIRST YEAR HOME

# Relearning

Relearning the art of living.

You will tell yourself you don't deserve happiness.
You'll whisper it to yourself in all those moments
where happiness should be all you feel.

If you Listen?

You'll be right.

# FIRST NIGHT

---

What did I lose, if not for the chance to be all those immeasurable things I wanted to be?

What did I lose, except for my ability to believe I could pass the test if my crucible were laid at my feet?

I lost my identity.

My sense of self evaporated as I awoke from ten hours of dreamless sleep drenched in piss. Seven months of fear without the opportunity to fight back climaxed with my body losing control of basic functions.

Fear gripped me so completely that when it released, I found myself in adult infancy. Relearning how to breath. Relearning how to sleep. Relearning how to live.

I lost me.

# ESCALATION

---

That fucking orange flag and its stupid pink back

Of all the things that could torture me, who thought
it'd be that?

It was powerless in life, even more so in my mind

I wave it and wave it and yet, each and every time

The flag waves frantic and my blood begins to chill

When I see that fucking car come over the hill

I know what happens next, but my brain has a surprise

It filled every dream with death, destruction, and lies

# NIGHTMARES

My desire for peace never eclipsed my capacity for violence. But in a split second I made the decision to not pull the trigger. It frightened me how much I wanted to. Knowing I could and harnessing the desire to do it was like chaining a rabid Cerberus to my soul forcing him to devour me instead. I could have ripped a burst through that windshield. The coward that led us wanted me to. Ordered me to. Told me I could have killed us all. But I didn't. And I still see their smiling faces and their waving hands driving by. And the horror of waiting for them to detonate has never left. It refuses to leave. I didn't let it kill them.

So now it's trying to kill me.

# DREAMER

Now I lay me down to sleep

I fear what thoughts my dreams will reap

This night and last and surely the next

I hide from my mind in a hole soul deep

I see their faces and I smell them bleed, pain
nonexistent where pain should be

Why can't the heart protect the mind from things the
eyes still see?

# MY TRIBE

My heart has felt empty since we disbanded our
disgruntled gang. I feared so much but nothing I
feared more than that day.

"FALL OUT!" to the world and go your separate ways.

Coming home was not a return to a familiar world.
We were exiled in our foreign land; we could speak the
language but knew you could not understand.

Unsure smiles and nervous laughter linger like an
exclamation point. The cruelty of a glimpse into what
life should be. There is no uncertainty when to love is
to bleed.

There was a time when I didn't fear death because of
me. I feared breathing my last and leaving my brothers
in need.

My family. My tribe.

For them I would have given everything. Then we
came back to a shallow puddle deep enough to make it
hard to breathe.

We're surrounded by people we can't even  trust to
say what they really mean, people who forget you as
quickly as if you disappeared from the news feed.

How are we supposed to survive here?

Separated from them.

Detached from myself.

I feel like a statistic, another talking point
of mental health.

A pariah.

A leper.

Alone because I can't recreate the surety of my tribe.

I want to love and be loved; I want to feel alive.

# GIVING HAND

Reach out they say

Reach out they write

Rest your worries here

And we'll help you fight

OK! I cheer with gratitude on my tongue

But the giving hand has already run

Nothing to say and nothing to write

So I whisper bitter nothings into the night

# TOO

Too sad

Too mad

Too bitter

Too undone

Too intense

Too in love

I'm too much

Of all of this.

Cut and run

Before you see

Just how much

You're just like me.

# NOT TONIGHT

If for nothing other than spite, I will make it through the night.

Nothing would insult me more than tribute and niceties from people who showed me no love in life.

I cling to that bitterness that accompanies a shoulder with a chip and I hide the words trying to explode from my lips

I may not be ok, but you won't get to see it beat me, you won't get to pretend like you cared.

Not tonight

# OPTIMISM

I used to think I was a kind, intelligent soul surrounded by dim wit and cruelty. It took far too long to realize I wasn't as clever as I thought and my benevolence only extended as far as your perceived usefulness to the world that revolved around me. Now I find myself at the edges of existence looking in at all the brilliant minds carving out their legacies in the halls of humanity and the hearts of their loved ones. Wishing, craving, pleading, begging for someone to drop spare love in my cup. I feel so alone standing at this bitter corner of life. Too afraid to stay here and too bitter to move along.

# 2AM

---

Fatigue makes you vulnerable. Lowers your ability
to react. Your eyes don't track and your ears hear the
noise behind it all, no matter how hard you strain.
Maybe that's why I write in darkness under sheets of
cotton grey. My heart no longer has the strength to
keep the pain locked away. Each tap of the screen is
a key that lets my demons out to play. Sad, Horny,
Broken, Lonely. Devils that never see the light of day.
Take advantage of heavy eyes and tell the truth behind
the lies. The roadmap to the battle lines that crisscross
through my brain. Me, myself, and I playing the most
dangerous game, lurking through the darkness to make
a trophy of my pain.

# WEEDS

---

If I die before my time, if I pass before my prime

Promise me, Promise me

Don't talk about it online

Where were you when I struggled, where were you
when I laughed?

Why are you here now that I've breathed my last?

Don't speak my name into the world if you didn't
first speak it to me

Don't use my absence to make up for yours

Don't use me to fulfill your notification need

It's funny how when a life ends,
friends pop up like weeds

# PERJURY

When it comes to the people in my past,

I know I've treated some better than others

But the ones we treat well aren't the ones who linger
on our minds in our quiet moments

When your brain interrogates your soul, you
remember each and every one of their names

Like stubborn stains that can't be bleached from
your conscience, each name a blotch
on the fabric of who you are

In those quiet moments, your soul takes the stand
and your brain whispers,

"Are you Good?"

Will you commit perjury in your own court?

# ROYALTY

If there's a god I'm sure he agrees

There's nothing good or worth preserving in me.

He chips me away chunk by chunk, relishing in my hastening decay.

I survived the month of May, but he knows it's a simple game of time.

Day after day I get closer to the finish line.

The end of the rope

The end of the barrel

The end of the fuck up

Christian the Miserable.

# COMPLIMENTS

I'm bitter and selfish and greedy to the core. But there's not enough self-deprecation to keep me from asking for more. So I'll plot and I'll scheme and I'll bend reality before I'm content with what I've got. Peek inside of me; try to ignore the decay. There used to be a golden heart nestled in that empty spot but it up and walked away:

It didn't fit in with the rot.

# SILENCE

I looked to the sky

And asked him why

Where's the lesson in wanting to die

Questioned again

To a mute reply

Silence the reward for staying alive

Pain the gift for daring to try

Dream of giving up

And bathing in the lake of fire

# MASOCHISM'S MELODY

Preach a good vibe a thousand times a day but I promise you it doesn't go away.

Preach a good line a thousand different ways but I promise you there's no truth in what you say.

I promise you there's a thousand thoughts that are all here to stay.

I promise you if you just accept it, it'd be better that way.

Faking a smile will never make it real.

Faking a laugh will never make you feel.

Understand, understand this, I preach to you.

There's a peace in learning to love the truth.

Not everyone is meant to smile.

# LEGACY

Today I wanted to kill myself and I came damn close.

There's no poetry in that.

No tragedy for the stage so you can feel bad for me and my never-ending sob story.

Just Reality.

Stark cold fact that I've found myself tiptoeing on the edge of completely giving up on this fuckin' life yet again.

And now I am faced with the barrage of guilt that I'm too weak to keep fighting this hard and anger that I've had to.

When's it going to stop?

Maybe that's my lot in life: to struggle and go nowhere but down.

Seemingly sinking as fast as how hard I fight against.

Quicksand that burns as you descend.

That's what life means to me.

# MIRROR

---

I am no longer afraid to look in the mirror. The reflection there knows no fear engulfed only in shame. Wasted time in a wasted life spent clawing at a goal no more real than the smile on my face. All is not well in the depths of me. Feet firmly on land but my soul long cast adrift. The doldrums of my mind offering no push, instead leaving me to rot within. I would reach to move my body away, but I wouldn't know where to lead it. My legs unmotivated and my mind doesn't care. All I can do is stand here and stare. I do not fear my reflection, but my reflection pities me.

# PROFILE PICTURE

Hippy hair, wire beard, wild eyed, broken ears. Hide my discolored smile behind cracked lips and cloak it in dry ill-treated skin hidden from sun. Painted with needles carried by cackling knees and popping ankles. Pain surpassed only by a bent spine that's curving more with time. A grotesque autobiography can't be complete without a cover picture of me far removed from what I'm supposed to be.

# ALONE

It's 1am and I'm a fiend for death again

Forget a pill and I've found myself on the edge again.

What do I say to not sound like I'm riding a generational trend?

Just another coward flirting with the end.

Now more than ever I need to stay alive, but it feels like I'll be the next casualty in the war with my mind.

The first to fall was happiness, closely followed by sadness.

Anger clung desperately to the satisfaction of the fight.

But that came to an end tonight.

My mind and I alone in the ring. If I were able to feel it, I'm sure it'd be a heart-wrenching thing.

My mind and I alone and I'm constantly reminded each time the bell dings.

To feel so alone is such a crippling thing.

# TASTE

I guess I'm just trying to recreate it.

The intensity of love, The reality of hate.

The clarity of life when death is in your face.

The adrenaline and passion I never thought I'd miss, have gone away and left the fear that lurks alone, cast adrift.

My terror craves its company, its companion of macabre bliss.

No rapture can be found in safety's insincere abyss.

No stranger bedfellows exist quite like you and I.

A lust for horror and pure ecstasy in staying alive.

I thought I found my war trapped in the taste of your lips, yet no taste is as temporary as that of a kiss.

So, hear this request from my fear and I:

Please let me recreate this until the day I die.

# BLIND

Undoubtably I've stumbled through the darkness,
reaching out halfheartedly for a support to catch me
from gracing the floor with my extended presence.

There's no denying I walked a path hidden from light
and screamed with liquor-filled lungs for someone,
anyone, to show me the way.

I will never escape the experience of not knowing if I'll
see the next day burning through the window.

# LANGUAGE BARRIER

When you speak of war, I hope you understand

There is nothing romantic about pools of blood in the sand

There is nothing attractive about choking on the mangled remnants of a jaw

There is nothing beautiful about the smell of human flesh being cooked by gasoline

There is nothing enviable about the things we endured and the things we saw

When you speak of war, I don't expect you to understand

When you speak of war, I'm glad you don't understand

But sometimes I wish you did

So that when I speak of war

I don't feel so misunderstood

# PUSH UPS

"Where'd the good ones go?" we ask

With a pistol to their skull

Die without reason

But write about a code

Come with me if you're not interested in shriveling until you're old.

# ON AND ON

Life doesn't stop when you feel it shatter in your chest.

No matter how much you wish it would.

Life doesn't rewind when you think of the thing you should have said and the thing you should have done.

Life moves forward and drags you with it, making sure to slam you against every mistake you've made along the way.

Life moves forward even if you're broken.

# LIGHT BLUE ROOM

I've thought about death constantly for so long, it wasn't until I was in that room that I realized it wasn't normal. The new norm was one foot in the grave and the other on ice and I saw nothing wrong with it. Now I'm at a crossroads. Death had become my personality. If I no longer wish for it, who am I?

I guess I'm alive.

# TRUTH

Now that I understand the why

I've figured out why it's become impossible to cry:

I expected to die.

A hero's death cloaked in glory.

Soaked in blood and one hell of a story,

but I lived.

I made it home after giving what my country asked me to give.

But I lived.

And nothing about that made me proud.

I didn't earn my place in hallowed ground.

And when the truth leaked through, that's when I knew.

I didn't expect to die:

I wanted to.

# HOLD

Carry on.

Carry on.

Hold fast until the break of day

Brave the storm and outlast the sea

Drown in the air around you and pray you remember
how to breathe

Stay strong, you lost soul, adrift and cast away

Stay alive.

Stay Alive.

There is no other way

No path exists to permanent blue skies. No road leads
to lasting green fields

But all calm seas are lost forever to the soul who yields

Hold fast until the break of day

Carry on.

Carry on.

I believe there's someone or something out there responsible for all of this, all of us, and all of our bullshit. I'm just pretty pissed off at whatever it is.

# AUTHOR'S NOTE

If you've made it this far, I want to thank you for allowing me to take you on a journey through my mind during some of my darkest moments. Now you've found yourself here with me on the other side and might be looking for a sign of hope. Something to tell you, "All is well".

The truth of it is, I, and many of my brothers and sisters in arms, have learned that these feelings do not always go away. They may dissipate with time, only for us to find them worse than we remembered. We may learn to cope with the feelings and carry them like a permanent new appendage, but they never truly disappear.

My nightmares about a seemingly innocuous event started while I was still in Helmand. A day where everyone involved walked away physically unscathed returns to me with exhausting regularity.

My poems are presented in a loosely chronological way so you can quite literally peer into how and when I was torturing myself. The why? Because I was too afraid to talk to my Marines, or anyone for that matter, about how I was feeling.

Guilt, shame, embarrassment, anger. I couldn't fathom going to the men I served with for help because I was certain they were all stronger and braver than I could ever be. After all, some of them had actually lived through an incredible amount more than even my worst nightmares.

I had bottled myself up so much and allowed it to get so bad that when I finally told the truth, I was sent to the emergency room. My desire to kill myself reached a point where I had made and acted on a plan to end my life.

But, as I am sure you have gathered, I am still here. I sought help, received my diagnoses and treatment plan, and every single day, I fight to overcome my symptoms.

The single most potent remedy I received, however, was my best friend confiding in me that he was feeling the same way. He understood me and my frustrations, and for the first time in an exceptionally long time, I didn't feel helpless. I wasn't ashamed. I wasn't alone.

That is why it is so crucially important to be heartachingly, gruesomely honest about the realities of what we feel. We do ourselves, and those to the left and right of us, a disservice by hiding away the pain we carry. Service members from the Global War on Terror are all too familiar with the phrase, "Check on your buddies". We all know that's only half the battle. Being honest about how you feel will save your life. It is ok to not be ok. You are not alone.

# THOUGHTS & SKETCHES

# THOUGHTS & SKETCHES

# THOUGHTS & SKETCHES

# THOUGHTS & SKETCHES

# THOUGHTS & SKETCHES

# THOUGHTS & SKETCHES

# THOUGHTS & SKETCHES

# THOUGHTS & SKETCHES

Corporal Christian Vanderbush
Lashkar Gah, Helmand Province,
Afghanistan, 2017

# About the Author

**Christian Vanderbush** was in the second grade on September 11th, 2001. He and thousands of others from his generation were forever impacted by that day and how the world changed in its wake. He would enlist to fight in the Global War on Terror that had started that day, and on July 29th, 2013, he found himself on the famed yellow footprints inside the gates of Marine Corps Recruit Depot San Diego.

He spent six years in the United States Marine Corps Reserve as an 0331 Machine Gunner. Most of it spent as Active Duty Operational Support engaging in community outreach and performing Funeral Honors for over 300 Marines and Marine Corps Veterans. In early 2017 the call went out for volunteers for a combat deployment to Afghanistan to support Operation Freedom's Sentinel, and he leaped at the chance.

After returning home from Afghanistan, Corporal Vanderbush served out the remainder of his obligatory service until spring 2019 and reentered the civilian world a changed man. He lives in Michigan with his wife, and they are expecting their first child, a son, in December. *Internal* is his maiden voyage into what he hopes will be a fulfilling career as a writer.

Lightning Source UK Ltd.
Milton Keynes UK
UKHW012308021220
374527UK00011B/888/J

9 780578 794464